PALEO SAUCES
SALAD DRESSINGS
DIPS
AND
MARANADES

By
LARRY HABER

Copyright 2013 by Feel Good Publications
All Rights Reserved
No part of this book may be reproduced in any manner without the express permission of the copyright
holder, except for small parts used for reviewing, quotations, and news purposes by appropriate organizations and persons

Table of Contents

Introduction

Chapter 1: The Basics
Yellow Mustard
Dijon Mustard
Basic Mayonnaise
Aioli
Ketchup
Sour Cream

Chapter 2: Marinades
Basic BBQ
Basic Greek
Ginger Lime
Asada
Balsamic
Strawberry Basil
Spicy Thai Coconut
Mango Chile
Tex-Mex Taco
Sweet Asian

Chapter 3: Classical Sauces
Hollandaise
Bearnaise
Bechamel
Au-Jus
Pesto

Chapter 4: Marinara
Basic Tomato Basil
Hearty Meaty
Roasted Pepper and Mushroom
Hot and Spicy
Four Cheese

Chapter 5: BBQ Sauce
Kansas City Style
Carolina Style Mustard Sauce
Louisiana Hot Sauce
Peach BBQ
Gourmet Coffee BBQ

Chapter 6: Cheese
Basic Cheddar
Spinach and Artichoke Dip

Nacho Cheese
Beefy Queso
White Wine and Swiss Fondue

Chapter 7: Mexican
Basic Salsa
Roasted Red Pepper Salsa
Salsa Verde
Guacamole
Chocolate Mole

Chapter 8: Dry Rubs and Spice Mixes
Basic BBQ
Tex-Mex Taco
Mediterranean Herb Crust
Asian Ginger
Spicy Chili

Chapter 9: Party Dips
Sour Cream and Onion
Multi-Nut Butter
Paleo Ranch Dip
Paleo Hummus
Pimento Cheese

Chapter 10: Salad Dressing
Ranch
Balsamic Vinaigrette
Greek
Zesty Italian
Caesar
Raspberry Vinaigrette
Strawberry Basil Balsamic Vinaigrette
Blueberry Thyme Vinaigrette
Green Goddess
Thai Coleslaw
Juicy Citrus
Thousand Island
Roasted Red Pepper
Ginger Almond
Honey Pecan

We live in a world of ultra-processed, vigorously marketed "food" products. Everything we eat these days comes in a box or a bag, and we usually consume it without a second thought to what evils might lurk therein. But a growing number of people have decided to break free from the artificiality of modern food and take a page from the book of our ancestors. These people follow the Primal Blueprint, commonly known as the Paleo diet.

This book is not exactly for people who are new to Paleo, but just in case this is the first Primal cookbook you've come across, let's take a look at what we mean when we say "Paleo".

The basic idea behind the Paleo way of life is that humans, on the whole, were healthier when our species was still in its infancy. Many of our most life-threatening diseases (like heart disease and cancer) simply didn't exist, and humans were generally leaner, more muscular and more physically fit. Part of this is because exercise was a matter of course, not an activity we had to "find the time for". Another major part is the fact that processed foods didn't exist; we ate what was fresh, local and hunted or foraged by our own hands.

The Paleo diet seeks to return – as much as possible – to these ways. While many of us don't have the time or wherewithal to hunt and forage our own food, it is possible to buy food that is produced in a more natural way; grass-fed or pastured meat, organic produce, and products that are made responsibly by producers that have the health of their consumers and the Earth in mind.

The benefits of Paleo are easy to see; increased overall health, more energy, and rapid weight loss for those who need it. The Paleo lifestyle also has a positive effect on our communities and the earth as a whole; encouraging responsible practices that leave out the harmful chemicals and encourage sustainable food production.

What is or isn't Paleo is a topic for another book (in fact, many books have already been filled with it!), and there are a few gray areas out there, but for the purposes of our journey here, Paleo means anything that humans could have hunted or foraged in the days before history. If you can imagine a caveman eating it, chances are it's Paleo.

Speaking of purposes, let's get down to ours!

One of the challenges of eating Paleo is that most people start out making food that is plain and unadorned. While healthy and admirable, this can get boring fast. You can only eat plain meat or veggies so many times before you're tempted to forsake your Paleo ideals and head to flavor town!

Luckily, the solution is not to accept defeat, but to up your game by building an arsenal of delicious, healthy, Paleo sauces, dips, salad dressings and marinades! A good sauce can change the character of an entire dish. Chicken is chicken, but with a fresh, healthy salsa it shimmies south of the border. Add a day of soaking in a primal BBQ sauce and suddenly you're out back by the grill. Take a boring bowl of lettuce and add some home made raspberry vinaigrette and you've got a refreshing, healthy lunch! Sauces, dips, salad dressings and marinades are the way we take the same beef, chicken and pork (let's face it, who can get elk, alligator or ostrich on a regular basis?) or even veggies, and make it unique every time you eat it.

In this book you will find your arsenal of sauces, dips salad dressings, marinades and even a dry rub or two. Some are basic; from Dijon mustard to a simple Greek marinade; some are a little more complicated; like our coffee BBQ. Some will have some similarities – variations on a theme – others will stand alone. All in all, this little book should keep your Paleo plate interesting long enough for you to become a creative master in your own right.

So without further ado, let's get saucy!

THE BASICS

Okay, down to business!

In this first chapter, we're going to cover five basic sauces that can not only be used as condiments in their own right, but will also serve as a base for future inventions. If you can master the five recipes outlined here, nothing in this book is out of your reach. The techniques used are the same techniques that go into making almost every sauce in this book.

Yellow Mustard

Everything begins with mustard. Mustard is the most basic condiment there is, and it is a vital ingredient in several of the most basic.

Yellow mustard might be America's favorite condiment. You'll find it on everything from burgers and hot dogs to tater tots and chili. Anywhere a tangy zip is needed, mustard is there. The making of yellow mustard seems mysterious to some, but in fact it's one of the easiest things you will ever make.

1 cup ground dry mustard seed (two of the little tins from the spice aisle ought to do it)
1 cup water
¾ cup white distilled vinegar
2 tsp tapioca flour
1 tsp salt
1/2 tsp turmeric
1/8 tsp garlic powder
1/8 tsp paprika

1. Combine all ingredients in a small pan over medium heat. Whisk until smooth.
2. When mixture comes to a boil, reduce heat to low and simmer 5 min.
3. Cover pan with a lid and allow to cool completely.
4. Chill in refrigerator before serving. Will stay fresh for months in the refrigerator.

Makes about 1 cup.

Dijon Mustard

If you're really a fan of mustard, you know nothing is quite like the hearty, tangy flavor of a good Dijon mustard. This powerful condiment forms a great base for salad dressings, and goes great on baked chicken or even lettuce-wrapped burgers.

1 cup ground dry mustard seed (two of the little tins from the spice aisle ought to do it)
1/2 cup water
¾ cup white wine vinegar
½ cup white wine
1 tsp salt
1/2 tsp turmeric
1/8 tsp garlic powder
2 tbsp minced shallot
¼ tsp ground coriander
pinch cumin

1. Combine all ingredients in a glass bowl and cover. Leave in refrigerator overnight
2. Transfer to a blender and blend until smooth.
3. Store in an airtight container in the fridge up to 2 weeks.

Makes about 2 cups.

Basic Mayonnaise

This mighty mayo makes use of Paleo-friendly cold-pressed grapeseed oil; a more neutral-flavored, stable alternative to extra virgin olive oil.

- 2 egg yolks
- 1 tbsp apple cider vinegar
- 1 tbsp lemon juice, or more to taste
- 1 tsp Dijon mustard
- 1 tsp salt, or more to taste
- 1½ cups grapeseed oil

1. In a large mixing bowl, combine egg yolks, vinegar, lemon juice, mustard and salt. Using an electric egg beater, beat until the mixture is slightly frothy.
2. Slowly at first, drip by tiny drip, whisk in the oil. What's happening here is the eggs and oil are creating a delicate emulsion. The mustard acts as a stabilizer, and grapeseed oil is pretty cooperative, but you want to go slow just in case, or your emulsion will break and you'll end up with something that looks like runny scrambled eggs swimming in oil. Not too pretty.
3. If your emulsion does break, never fear. The easy fix is to crack a fresh egg yolk in a new bowl and slowly, drip by drip add the broken mixture into it as you whisk vigorously – just as you should have the first time!
4. As your emulsion builds, it will become more stable and you can begin to add the oil faster. In the end, your mayo should be a creamy off-white with a velvery texture, creamy flavor and a tart zing to it.

Makes about 1 pint.

Aioli

Technically, aioli is just a mayonnaise that uses olive oil as the fat and mashed roasted garlic as the emulsifier. Olive oil is a bit more temperamental than grapeseed, so be sure to take this one slow! The flavor is pungently continental, and goes good with everything from burgers to veggies to home made chips.

- 2 egg yolks
- 4-6 large cloves of roasted garlic, mashed into a paste
- 2 tbsp lemon juice
- 2 tsp salt
- 1 cup extra virgin olive oil

1. In a large mixing bowl, combine egg yolks, lemon juice, garlic paste and salt. Using an electric egg beater, beat until the mixture is slightly frothy.
2. Slowly, drip by tiny drip, add the olive oil. We cannot stress enough that you must go slow with aioli! Garlic is a great emulsifier, but it is not an infinitely stable one, and you can overtax it if you rush this process! Don't get all gung-ho when you see the emulsion coming together quickly, this one is worth taking your time.
3. When you've added all the oil, the aioli will be a similar texture to the mayo, with a more pungent olive oil and garlic flavor. Stirring in fresh herbs and spices is highly recommended to make this condiments shine.

Makes about 1½ cups.

Ketchup

Another American behemoth, ketchup is another one of those condiments we put on everything. Burgers, dogs, potatoes, eggs, you name it, we love our sweet and tangy ketchup. For us Paleo people, however, the traditional molasses and sugar are not a feasible possibility, so we have to make do with the natural sweetness of tomato paste (a Paleo-friendly product) and add just the right concoction of spices to approximate that familiar flavor as best we can.

2 6 oz. cans of tomato paste
¼ cup apple cider vinegar
½ tsp ground dry mustard
2/3 cup water
½ tsp cinnamon
¼ tsp ground clove
¼ tsp ground allspice
¼ tsp ground nutmeg
1/8 tsp cayenne

1. In a small mixing bowl, whisk together all ingredients until well combined.
2. Leave in refrigerator overnight for flavors to develop.

Makes about 1 cup.

Sour Cream

Some dishes just aren't complete without a touch of sour cream. This creative substitution makes it Paleo!

1 14 oz. can full-fat coconut milk
1-2 tbsp lemon juice or apple cider vinegar
¼ tsp salt

1. Leave the can of coconut milk in the refrigerator overnight. The cream will separate from the milk and harden.
2. Open the can from the BOTTOM. This allows you to pour out the milk and leaves you with only the fat.
3. Scoop the fat into a small mixing bowl.
4. Stir in lemon juice or vinegar and salt. Taste, add more if desired.
5. Serve wherever you would normally serve sour cream!

Makes about 1 cup.

MARINADES

Marinades are another basic foundation that will make your Paleo plate more exciting. Even if you eat a pretty healthy variety of meats, chances are that beef, chicken and pork are staples in your diet. Though each animal has a number of cuts that can provide different flavors, in the end, it's really only three meats – and that can get boring! Marinating your meat in a variety of concoctions can help you break the monotony, and show your friends and family what a creative chef you are!

Essentially, all a marinade does is break down the tissues in your meat. This is achieved by the presence of something acidic, usually vinegar or citrus, but many fruits also work. As the marinade breaks down and seeps into the meat, it brings whatever flavors are near with it, so you want to pack these marinades with as much flavor as you can! Once you've tried a few, feel free to get inventive and make up your own creations!

Basic BBQ Marinade

Traditionally, BBQ flavor is imparted with a spicy dry rub, a robust sauce and a good long stay in a well-seasoned smoker. But if you lack any of those three ingredients, this simple marinade will get you pretty close.

- 3 cloves garlic
- ½ onion, diced
- ½ cup, plus 2 tbsp grapeseed oil
- ¼ cup applesauce
- ¼ cup apple cider vinegar
- ¼ cup coconut aminos
- 1 tbsp lemon juice
- 1 tbsp salt
- 1 tbsp smoked paprika
- 2 tsp roasted ground cumin
- 2 tsp roasted coriander seed
- 2 tsp chipotle chili powder
- 1 tsp ground mustard
- 1 tsp sage
- 1 tsp celery seed
- 1 tsp black pepper

1. Sautee the garlic and onion in the 2 tbsp of oil for about 6-7 min, until slightly charred.
2. Add all ingredients to a food processor and blend until smooth.
3. Pour over meat in a zip-top bag or airtight container.
4. Marinate at least 4 hours, up to 2 days.

Makes enough for 2 lbs of meat.

Basic Greek Marinade

This simple, herbaceous marinade goes great on chicken or pork. It adds a tangy flavor that's perfect for cool summer salads or healthy shish-kabobs with red peppers an zucchini.

- ½ cup olive oil
- ¼ cup white wine vinegar
- ¼ cup fresh basil, packed
- 2 tbsp fresh oregano, packed

1 tbsp fresh thyme
3 cloves garlic
1 tsp black pepper
1 tsp salt

1. Add all ingredients to a food processor and blend until smooth.
2. Pour over meat in a zip-top bag or airtight container.
3. Marinate at least 4 hours, up to 2 days.

Makes enough for 1-2 pounds of meat.

Ginger Lime Marinade

Here's a spicy marinade that goes great on southeast Asian dishes. Perfect for pork, beef or chicken, the hot and tangy flavor will send any dish into the stratosphere!

½ cup grapeseed oil
juice of ½ orange
juice and zest of 1 lime
1 tbsp grated fresh ginger
1 tsp salt
1 tsp black pepper

1. Mix all ingredients in a mixing bowl until well combined.
2. Pour over meat in a zip-top bag or airtight container.
3. Marinate at least 4 hours up to 2 days.

Makes enough for 1 pound of meat.

Asada Marinade

The classic Mexican marinated meat, Pollo or Carne Asada is the perfect summer grill meal. Served by itself or in a lettuce wrap, it's a Paleo masterpiece that you'll want to make again and again!

½ onion, diced
3 cloves garlic
1 jalapeno, sliced
½ cup plus 2 tbsp olive oil
1 tbsp apple cider vinegar
juice and zest of 1 lime
juice and zest of 1 lemon
juice and zest of 1 orange
¼ cup fresh cilantro, packed
2 tbsp roasted ground cumin
1 tsp chipotle chili powder
1 tsp roasted coriander seed
1 tsp salt
1 tsp black pepper

1. Sautee the onion, garlic and jalapeno in the 2 tbsp oil, about 6-8 min, until well charred.
2. Add all ingredients to a food processor and blend until smooth.

3. Pour over meat in a zip-top bag or airtight container
4. Marinate at least 4 hours, up to 2 days.

Makes enough for 2 lbs of meat.

Balsamic Marinade

The sweet and tart flavor of balsamic vinegar is a welcome addition to pork, beef or even chicken. Combined with a blast of fresh herbs, this marinade will give your dish a hearty continental flair.

½ cup olive oil
¼ cup balsamic vinegar
¼ cup fresh basil, packed
2 tbsp fresh thyme
2 tbsp fresh oregano
2 tbsp fresh tarragon
1 tbsp fresh rosemary
4 cloves garlic
2 tsp salt
1 tsp black pepper

1. Add all ingredients to a food processor and blend until smooth.
2. Pour ingredients over meat in a zip-top bag or airtight container.
3. Marinate at least 4 hours, up to 2 days.

Makes enough for 1-2 pounds of meat.

Strawberry Basil Marinade

If you're looking for a sweeter twist for your next chicken dish, try this sweet and herbaceous marinade. Excellent on salads, kabobs and by itself!

1 cup fresh sliced strawberries
½ cup grapeseed oil
juice and zest of 1 lemon
¼ cup basil, packed
1 tsp salt
1 tsp black pepper

1. Blend all ingredients in a food processor until smooth.
2. Pour over meat in a zip-top bag or airtight container
3. Marinate at least 4 hours, up to 2 days.

Spicy Thai Coconut Marinade

This creamy and spicy Asian marinade will take your next chicken or pork dish to a completely new place. With a winning combination of fresh jalapeno, basil and coconut milk, it's delightfully different!

½ cup coconut milk
½ cup water

2 tbsp coconut oil, melted and slightly cooled
2 jalapenos
½ cup fresh basil (Thai basil, of you can get it)
1 tsp salt
1 tsp dried ginger

1. Place all ingredients in a food processor and blend until smooth.
2. Pour over meat in a zip-top bag or airtight container
3. Marinate at least 2 hours, up to 1 day.

Makes enough for 1-2 pounds of meat.

Mango Chile Marinade

This sweet and spicy concoction is a different twist on standard Latin fare. Drawing more from South American influences than Mexican, it's sure to wow whoever you serve it to! Great on beef, chicken and pork.

3 dried chile peppers
½ cup beef or chicken stock (depending on what meat you're using)
1 very ripe mango, peeled and sliced
1 Serrano pepper, sliced
¼ onion, diced
Juice of 1 lemon
1 tbsp fresh cilantro, chopped
1 tsp cumin
1 tsp chipotle chili powder
1 tsp coriander
1 tsp salt
1 tsp black pepper

1. In a small sauce pot, bring the stock to a boil.
2. Slice the dried chiles and remove the stems and seeds.
3. Reduce heat to low and rehydrate the chiles in the broth, about 5-6 min.
4. Pull chiles out and discard broth.
5. Add all remaining ingredients to a food processor and blend until smooth.
6. Pour over meat in a zip-top bag or airtight container.
7. Marinate at least 2 hours, up to 1 day.

Makes enough for 2 pounds of meat.

Tex-Mex Taco Marinade

Designed for quick and easy marinating on a week night, this simple Tex-Mex flavor will give any meat a kick in the pants!

½ cup grapeseed oil
¼ cup apple cider vinegar
2 tbsp lemon juice
2 tsp garlic powder
2 tsp dried onion (or ¼ fresh onion, diced)

2 tsp cumin
1 tsp coriander
1 tsp cayenne
1 tsp salt
1 tsp black pepper
½ tsp red pepper flake

1. Mix all ingredients well in a mixing bowl.
2. Pour over meat in a zip-top bag or airtight container.
3. Marinate at least 2 hours, up to 2 days.

Makes enough for 1 pound of meat.

Sweet Asian Marinade

There's really nothing quite like Teriyaki, and this sweet and tangy Asian-inspired marinade gets that special flavor, but keeps it all natural. Sesame oil is a Paleo gray area, but any negative health effects (which are mild anyway) are mitigated by the small amount used.

1 very ripe peach, peeled and sliced
¼ cup cucumber, sliced, peeled and seeds removed
¼ cup coconut aminos
2 tbsp sesame oil
1 tbsp lemon juice
2 cloves garlic, minced
2 tsp salt
1 tsp black pepper
1 tsp fresh ginger, grated
¼ tsp ground clove
¼ tsp ground allspice

1. Add all ingredients to a food processor and blend until smooth. (If you have a juicer, juice the cucumber first and use only the juice.)
2. Pour over meat in a zip-top bag or airtight container.
3. Marinate at least 4 hours, up to 1 day.

Makes enough for 1-2 pounds of meat.

CLASSICAL SAUCES

In this chapter we're going to give you a few trick to make five of the most universally revered classical gourmet sauces. Some are pretty close to Paleo on their own, others need a little love before they fit into the Paleo lifestyle.

These sauces (with the exception of pesto) all form the base for a family of sauces that you can use to reproduce some of your favorite dishes. From eggs Benedict to steak Oscar, learning these sauces will open up a world of continental fare for you and your family!

Hollandaise

Hollandaise is a lot like a warm mayo, just using clarified butter as the fat instead of oil. It's an emulsion, and it's subject to the same finicky issues as most emulsions. Luckily, proper heating makes this one easy enough, and it's already Paleo without any help. Store-bought Hollandaise, however, will be thickened with everything from wheat flour to cellulose powder (sawdust, essentially!), so make it at home! It's fun, easy and delicious!

2 egg yolks
½ cup coconut oil, melted
1 tbsp lemon juice
1 pinch salt
1 pinch cayenne

1. Fill a medium sauce pot with about 1" of water. Bring to a boil.
2. Place a glass bowl over the boiling water to make a double boiler.
3. Add egg yolks, lemon juice, salt and cayenne to glass bowl and whisk until slightly foamy.
4. Reduce heat to low.
5. Melt coconut oil in the microwave.
6. Slowly, drip by drip, add the coconut oil, whisking constantly. (Just as you would with oil in a mayo recipe)
7. When you've added all the coconut oil, remove from heat and continue to whisk for about 30 seconds to ensure the emulsion is stable.
8. Serve hot over eggs, meat or vegetables – it's good on everything!

Makes about ½ cup.

Bearnaise

Bearnaise is a cousin of Hollandaise that adds additional flavor through a white wine and vinegar reduction. That may sound fancy, but all a reduction is is a liquid that's been left to boil for a little while. It's basically another step added to Hollandaise that brings the flavor to a more tangy, robust place. Traditionally served on meats.

For the reduction:
¼ cup white wine vinegar
¼ cup dry white wine
1 tsp minced shallot
2 tbsp dried tarragon
¼ tsp black pepper
1 pinch salt

For the sauce:

3 egg yolks
2 tbsp cold coconut oil
½ cup melted coconut oil
1 tbsp fresh tarragon, chopped

1. In a small sauce pan, combine all the reduction ingredients.
2. Bring to a boil and allow to reduce, stirring frequently, until only about 2 tbsp of liquid remain. Allow to cool slightly.
3. Fill a medium sauce pot with 1" of water and bring to a boil.
4. In a glass bowl, whisk egg yolks until frothy.
5. Add the cooled reduction to the eggs slowly, whisking constantly. Do not add too fast or the eggs will cook.
6. Whisk the cold coconut oil into the egg mixture.
7. Place the glass bowl atop the pot of boiling water and whisk vigorously until everything is incorporated.
8. Slowly, drip by drip, add the melted coconut oil.
9. When all coconut oil is incorporated, remove from heat and whisk in the fresh tarragon.
10. Serve over steak and asparagus to make classic steak Oscar.

Makes about ¾ cup.

Bechamel

Bechamel is the basic white sauce you'd find in any European gourmet restaurant. It's used for so many things it's hard to list them all; soups, cheese sauces, casseroles, pasta dishes, you name it. And because it usually includes flour, it's off the Paleo menu.

No more! This tricky little recipe uses our old friend the coconut (where would we be without coconuts?) to substitute for several ingredients. The result is a deliciously light and creamy sauce that you can use on, well, anything!

1 can (14 oz.) coconut milk
2 tbsp coconut flour
2 tbsp coconut oil
2 tsp salt

1. Melt coconut oil to a medium sauce pot.
2. Add coconut flour and stir into a roux. Flour should slightly brown in the oil.
3. Add coconut milk and whisk vigorously
4. Add salt and boil for 10 minutes, stirring constantly.
5. Serve over cauliflower or broccoli for a creamy addition to your veggie sides, or incorporate into a Paleo redux of a classical dish!

Makes about 1½ cups.

Au-Jus

If you've ever had a great prime rib or a French dip, you know Au-Jus. It's that beefy, fatty, runny sauce that makes everything deliciously savory. Luckily for us, it's pretty close to Paleo to begin with, all it needs is one little flour substitution and you're off and running!

¼ cup of beef fat drippings

2 cups beef broth
1½ tbsp tapioca flour
salt and pepper to taste

1. Melt beef fat in a pan.
2. Stir in tapioca flour, whisking vigorously, until mixture thickens, about 2-3 min.
3. Add beef broth.
4. Boil mixture until it thickens slightly.
5. Season with salt and pepper.
6. Serve with roast beef, of course!

Makes about 2 cups.

Pesto

Pesto is that heavenly herb-based sauce that goes great on everything from beef to fish. It's dead simple to make, and a great way to make use of extra herbs you have lying around. Traditional pesto (which is what we're making) is mostly made up of basil, but there's no reason you can't make it with parsley, tarragon, oregano, or any of your favorite fresh herbs. Add some onions and cilantro, remove the nuts and you have chimichurri. It's a basic approach that can produce a multitude of amazing sauces.

2 cups fresh basil, packed
½ cup olive oil
¼ cup plus 1 tbsp pine nuts
3-4 cloves garlic
½ tsp salt
½ tsp black pepper

1. Place all ingredients in a food processor and blend until smooth.
2. Serve over beef, shredded zucchini pasta or fried squash!

Makes about 2 cups.

MARINARA

Some of you might have skimmed through the last chapter and thought to yourself "What? No tomato sauce?" Never fear, we didn't forget! It's just that there are so many great ways to prepare marinara that we thought we'd devote an entire chapter to it!

Marinara is the quintessential Italian spin on tomato based sauces, and it's definitely one of the core sauces of European cuisine. Luckily for us Paleo people, when made fresh at home, marinara is already approved! That's why we've chosen to present this wonderful sauce as it's own chapter – so we can give you an idea of the humongous potential this sauce has.

Spread any of these on chicken, beef or thinly sliced veggies for a taste of Italy!

Basic Tomato Basil

First, let's hit the basics. In it's simplest form, marinara is cooked, seasoned tomatoes, and that's all this little sauce is.

12-14 large roma or plum tomatoes, quartered
2 tbsp olive oil
½ onion, diced
2 cloves garlic, minced
¼ cup fresh basil, chopped
2 tbsp fresh parsley, chopped
1 tsp salt
1 tsp black pepper

1. In a large pot, sautee the garlic and onion in oil until soft, about 3 min.
2. Add the tomatoes and allow to cook, stirring frequently, until tomatoes are soft, about 10 min.
3. Add herbs and seasonings, cook an additional 5 min.
4. Transfer sauce to a blender or food processor and blend until smooth.
5. Return to pot and allow to simmer over low heat, stirring frequently, until sauce reaches desired thickness, up to 30 min.
6. Serve over shredded zucchini pasta or Paleo meatloaf!

Makes about 2 quarts.

Hearty Meaty Marinara

This sauce builds on the basic marinara to make a thick and meaty sauce that is a meal in itself! Serve with cooked vegetables for a one-dish dinner!

12-14 large roma or plum tomatoes, quartered
2 tbsp olive oil
½ onion, diced
2 cloves garlic, minced
2 tbsp fresh parsley, chopped
1 tsp dried oregano
1 tsp dried thyme
1 tsp salt
1 tsp black pepper
1 lb ground beef
½ cup beef stock

1. Brown the beef in a pan. Set aside.
2. In a large pot, sautee garlic and onion in oil until soft, about 3 min.
3. Add the tomatoes and allow to cook, stirring frequently, until tomatoes are soft, about 10 min.
4. Add herbs and seasonings, cook an additional 5 min.
5. Transfer sauce to a blender or food processor and blend until smooth.
6. Return sauce to pot and add beef broth. Allow to cook until sauce reduces by about ¼, stirring frequently, about 10-15 min.
7. Stir in beef.
8. Cook for 5 more min.
9. Serve hot over spaghetti squash or pureed root vegetables!

Makes about 2 ½ quarts.

Roasted Pepper and Mushroom Marinara

This delicious veggie delight goes great on anything where tomatoes are welcome, including beef and pork chops!

1 red bell pepper
1 green bell pepper
12-14 large roma or plum tomatoes, quartered
2 tbsp olive oil
½ onion, diced
2 cloves garlic, minced
½ cup mushrooms, sliced
¼ cup fresh basil, chopped
¼ cup fresh parsley, chopped
2 tsp salt
1 tsp black pepper

1. Roast the peppers in the oven for 10-15 min, until nicely charred.
2. Under cool running water, peel the skin off the peppers and remove stems, ribs and seeds. Set aside.
3. In a large pot, sautee garlic and onion until soft, about 3 min.
4. Add the tomatoes and allow to cook, stirring frequently, until tomatoes are soft, about 10 min.
5. Add peppers, herbs and seasonings, allow to cook an additional 5 min.
6. Transfer sauce to a blender or food processor, blend until smooth.
7. Return to Pan and add mushrooms. Cook for an additional 10 min, until mushrooms are soft.
8. Serve with your favorite veggies or chicken cutlets!

Make about 2½ quarts.

Hot and Spicy Marinara

Sometimes you want your tomato sauce to have a little kick, and sometimes you want a lot! This spicy sauce is not for the faint of heart.

12-14 large roma or plum tomatoes, quartered
2 tbsp olive oil
1 small onion, diced
7-8 cloves garlic, minced
1 jalapeno, sliced
¼ cup fresh parsley, chopped
1 tsp red pepper flake
1 tsp paprika
1 tsp salt
1 tsp black pepper
½ tsp cayenne

1. In a large pot, sautee the onion, garlic and jalapeno until nicely charred, about 5-8 min.
2. Add the tomatoes and allow to cook, stirring frequently, until tomatoes are soft, about 10 min.
3. Add herbs and seasonings, allow to cook an additional 5 min.
4. Transfer sauce to a blender or food processor, blend until smooth.
5. Return sauce to pot and simmer over medium heat for an additional 10 min.
6. Serve with homemade Italian sausage or spicy meatballs!

Makes about 2 quarts.

Four Cheese Marinara

Cheese may be a Paleo gray area, but for those of you who do tolerate dairy this book would be incomplete without a cheesy marinara recipe!

12-14 large roma or plum tomatoes, quartered
2 tbsp olive oil
½ onion, diced
2 cloves garlic, minced
2 tbsp fresh parsley, chopped
1 tsp salt
1 tsp black pepper
¼ cup grated Parmesan
¼ cup grated Romano
¼ cup shredded white cheddar
¼ cup shredded mozzarella

1. In a large pot, sautee the garlic and onion in oil until soft, about 3 min.
2. Add the tomatoes and allow to cook, stirring frequently, until tomatoes are soft, about 10 min.
3. Add herbs and seasonings, cook an additional 5 min.
4. Transfer sauce to a blender or food processor and blend until smooth.
5. Return to pot and allow to simmer over low heat.
6. Add cheeses, stirring vigorously.
7. Stirring constantly, allow to simmer over low heat for an additional 5 min.
8. Serve with fried zucchini or over veggie pasta!

Makes about 2 quarts.

BBQ SAUCE

BBQ sauce has been a friend to meat since time immemorial. The robust, smoky flavor just delivers something you can't get from any other condiment, and it makes any meat feel right at home on the grill.

The problem for Paleo eaters is that most store-bought BBQ sauces are loaded with processed sugar and other artificial nastiness that we just don't want. You can make BBQ at home easily enough, but still, most recipes will call for sugar, molasses, whiskey – things we don't need in our diet!

Presented here are five creative solutions to approximate that classic BBQ flavor, without all the nonsense.

Kansas City Style BBQ Sauce

Kansas city is known nationwide for a sweeter, thicker sauce, but if you go there you'll find that the town favorites tend to be more balanced sauces with a good amount of kick. All the oldest, most established BBQ joints serve it up nice and spicy, without too much sweetness. This recipe attempts to find that balance.

- 3 6 oz. cans tomato paste
- ½ cup water
- ½ cup applesauce
- ¼ cup apple cider vinegar
- ¼ cup coconut aminos
- 1 tbsp lemon juice
- 1 tbsp smoked paprika
- 2 tsp roasted ground cumin
- 2 tsp chipotle chili powder
- 2 tsp roasted coriander
- 1 tsp red pepper flake
- 1 tsp ground mustard
- 1 tsp ground sage
- 1 tsp celery seed
- ½ tsp cayenne
- ½ tsp ground cloves
- ½ tsp ground cinnamon

1. In a large pot, whisk together all ingredients over medium heat.
2. Allow to simmer for 20 minutes, stirring frequently.
3. Brush over meats while on the grill, or serve as a dipping sauce!

Makes about 2 cups.

Carolina Style Mustard Sauce

In the Carolinas there are about as many types of BBQ sauce as there are towns. Nowhere in the country are regional tastes so different and so hotly contested. This mustard-based BBQ is one of the most well known, and one of the tastiest.

- 2 cups yellow mustard
- ½ cup apple cider vinegar
- 3 tbsp tomato paste
- ½ tsp chipotle chili powder

½ cup apple sauce
½ cup strong chicken broth (reduce it from 1 cup to concentrate the flavor)
2 tbsp dried rosemary
3 tsp ground mustard
2 tsp onion powder
2 tsp garlic powder
1 tsp celery seed
1 tsp salt
1 tsp black pepper

1. Mix all ingredients together in a mixing bowl.
2. Use as a baste when grilling pork or chicken, and as a finishing sauce at the table.

Makes about 3 ½ cups.

Louisiana Style Hot Sauce

Down on the bayou, anything that goes on the grill is BBQ and all of it gets hot sauce. This classic sauce goes good on everything from beef brisket to fish, and you'll impress anyone you serve it to.

2 red bell peppers
½ very ripe peach, peeled
½ cup apple cider vinegar
3 cloves of garlic
2 tbsp chipotle chili powder
3 tbsp tomato paste
1 pinch salt

1. Preferably on a charcoal grill (but in the oven would be okay) roast the red peppers and the peach until they are well charred. Pepper will take around 10 minutes, peach might be done in as little as 5.
2. Add all ingredients to a blender or food processor and blend until smooth.
3. If possible, bottle it and add to any grilled meat you desire!

Makes about 2 cups.

Peach BBQ Sauce

If you're looking for a classic, sweet BBQ like what you'd find in the store, this is the recipe for you. Here we've stripped out most of the heat and replaced it with a healthy dose of natural fruit for that sweet and savory flavor.

1 very ripe peach, peeled and sliced
½ onion, diced
2 cloves garlic, minced
2 tbsp grapeseed oil
2 6 oz. cans tomato paste
½ cup water
¼ cup coconut aminos
¼ cup apple cider vinegar
2 tbsp lemon juice

2 tbsp smoked paprika
1 tbsp roasted ground cumin
1 tbsp ground mustard
1 tsp celery seed
1 tsp ground sage

1. In a large skillet, sautee the peaches, garlic and onions until slightly charred, about 5-7 min.
2. Add all ingredients to a blender or food processor and blend until smooth.
3. Serve with fish, chicken, pork, you name it!

Makes about 2 cups.

Gourmet Coffee BBQ Sauce

Coffee is a common ingredient in gourmet BBQ sauces – the kind you might find at restaurants whose head chef is on Food Network. This deceptively simple ingredient adds a whole new layer of body and depth to the BBQ sauce, making it the perfect compliment for those high-end meats we Paleo people sometimes treat ourselves to.

2 6 oz. cans tomato paste
½ onion, diced
2 cloves garlic, minced
2 tbsp grapeseed oil
½ cup very strong brewed coffee
¼ cup apple cider vinegar
¼ cup coconut aminos
1 tbsp smoked paprika
2 tsp roasted ground cumin
2 tsp chipotle chili powder
2 tsp roasted coriander
1 tsp ground mustard
1 tsp ground sage
1 tsp celery seed

1. In a pan, sautee garlic and onions in the oil until slightly charred, about 5-7 min.
2. Add all ingredients to a blender or food processor and blend until smooth.
3. Serve with hearty game meats like elk, boar or venison.

Makes about 2 cups.

CHEESE SAUCE

As previously stated, cheese is a Paleo gray area. Some writers out there in the blogosphere decry the eating of cheese on a Paleo diet, others include it in their recipes without so much as an explanation of why it's okay.

The most agreed upon principle, however, is that you eat what you can tolerate. Some people bloat up when they walk by a cheese-filled deli case. Others can eat it by the block and still lose weight. Whichever you are, just do what works for you, and remember, there's always the trusted 80/20 rule: be good 80% of the time and you'll probably be alright.

That said, there are a few yummy, classic cheese sauces that a book about sauce would be remiss to... well, miss!

Basic Cheddar Sauce

This is the sauce we would use on mac and cheese, if we ate macaroni noodles. It's great on broccoli and cauliflower, as well as chicken, burgers and more!

1 cup heavy cream
8 oz shredded sharp cheddar (shred from a block to avoid additives)
1-2 tbsp tapioca flour (optional)
½ tsp Dijon mustard
1 pinch salt
1 pinch black pepper, if desired

1. In a medium sauce pot, bring the cream to a boil, whisking constantly to avoid boiling over.
2. Whisk in Dijon, salt and pepper.
3. Add cheese a handful at a time, whisking constantly.
4. Simmer for 5-10 minutes, until sauce thickens. If sauce doesn't seem to be thickening, add tapioca flour a little at a time, whisking constantly.
5. Once you have the desired consistency, pour it over your favorite veggies or a nice, nut-crusted chicken filet!

Makes about 1 cup.

Spinach and Artichoke Dip

We may not eat corn chips, but that doesn't mean we don't occasionally crave a little spinach and artichoke dip! Luckily the veggies in question are already in our wheelhouse, so all we need to do is make sure the saucy part is up to code!

1 small can artichoke hearts
2 cups spinach
2 tbsp olive oil
1 cup heavy cream
4 oz shredded Parmesan, plus extra for sprinkling
4 oz shredded mozzarella
1 tsp Dijon mustard
1-2 tbsp tapioca flour (optional)
1 tsp black pepper
1 pinch salt

1. In a pan, sautee the spinach and artichoke hearts until the spinach has fully reduced and the

artichoke hearts are slightly browned, about 5-7 min.
2. In a separate pan, bring cream to a boil, whisking constantly to avoid boiling over.
3. Whisk in Dijon, salt and pepper.
4. Add cheese a handful at a time, whisking constantly.
5. Simmer for 5-10 minutes, until sauce thickens. If sauce doesn't seem to be thickening, add tapioca flour a little at a time, whisking constantly.
6. When sauce is thick, stir in spinach and artichokes.
7. Top with shredded Parmesan and serve with raw zucchini and carrots for dipping.

Makes about 2 cups.

Nacho Cheese

When most people think of nacho cheese, they are unable to separate it from the plastic peel-top container it comes in. This recipe gives it to you all natural Paleo style.

2 tbsp clarified butter
2 tbsp tapioca flour
1 cup heavy cream
8 oz shredded mild cheddar or colby
½ tsp chili powder
pickled jalapenos on the side

1. In a medium pot, melt butter.
2. Add tapioca flour, whisking vigorously.
3. Pour in heavy cream and bring to a simmer.
4. Add cheese a handful at a time, whisking constantly.
5. Sprinkle in chili powder.
6. Serve over Mexican marinated beef or with veggies for dipping!

Makes about 1 cup.

Beefy Queso Dip

While we're on the subject of Mexican cheese dips, why not throw in a nice, beefy queso for good measure? Great with almond flour chips or fresh veggies!

¼ lb ground beef
1 tbsp diced onion
1 clove garlic, minced
2 tbsp diced tomatoes
1 tbsp diced pickled jalapenos
2 tbsp clarified butter
2 tbsp tapioca flour
1 cup heavy cream
8 oz shredded sharp cheddar

1. In a pan, brown the beef with the onions and garlic.
2. In a medium sauce pan, melt butter.
3. Add tapioca flour, whisking vigorously.
4. Pour in heavy cream and bring to a simmer.

5. Add cheese a handful at a time, whisking constantly.
6. Add beef, onions, garlic tomatoes and jalapenos.
7. Allow to cook 5 min, stirring constantly.
8. Serve with seasoned almond flour chips or pour over cooked veggies for a hearty Mexican side.

Makes about 1½ cups.

White Wine and Swiss Fondue

If you're throwing a fancy party, one sure-fire way to impress you guests is to whip out the fondue pot. Even if you don't have one, you can easily imitate it's gentle cooking style in a double boiler.

8 oz. shredded Swiss cheese
8 oz. shredded Gruyere cheese
4 tbsp tapioca flour
1 clove garlic, peeled
1 cup dry white wine
1 tbsp lemon juice
½ tsp ground mustard
1 pinch nutmeg

1. In a mixing bowl, toss shredded cheeses with tapioca flour.
2. Rub the inside of your fondue pot or double boiler with garlic, then discard the clove.
3. Over medium heat, add the wine and lemon juice and bring to a simmer.
4. Add the cheese a handful at a time, whisking constantly.
5. Once the fondue is smooth, stir in the ground mustard and nutmeg.
6. Serve with apples, carrots and jicama for dipping.

Serves 4-8.

MEXICAN

Some of our favorite sauces and dips come from south of the border, and we Paleo people should have nothing to fear when it comes to our favorite Mexican dishes. Many of them are based on the fresh fruits, vegetables and herbs native to the region, and are therefore easy to produce naturally in your kitchen.

We already covered queso in the cheese chapter, so you won't find that here. What you will find are three very different salsa recipes that are bound to spice up any party or Latin cuisine, one guacamole recipe that will knock your socks off, and a special chocolate mole recipe that only the more daring among us will attempt.

All in all, Latin food is sounding pretty good!

Basic Salsa

Salsa can be so many things it's hard to really put a finger on it. The Spanish word really just means "sauce" so in Spanish it literally can be anything! In America, and most of the world, however, we think of that chunky, spicy tomato-based dip that keeps begging for another bowl of corn chips. The chips might not be Paleo, but the salsa is!

6 large roma or plum tomatoes, quartered
¼ onion, diced
1 clove garlic, minced
¼ cup fresh cilantro
1 jalapeno, diced (if you like it hot, leave the seeds and ribs, if not take them out)
juice of 1/2 lime
1 tsp cumin
1 tsp salt
1 tsp black pepper

1. Add all ingredients to a blender or food processor and blend to desired texture. For chunky salsa, pulse for 30 seconds. For thin salsa, blend on high for 1 minute.
2. Serve with raw veggies, almond flour chips or on Pollo Asada!

Makes about 1 quart.

Roasted Red Pepper Salsa

This roasty-toasty variation on our classic salsa will keep everybody guessing how you pulled it off!

2 red bell peppers
2 large roma or plum tomatoes, quartered
2 tbsp olive oil
½ onion, cut in large chunks
1 jalapeno, halved, stem removed
juice of 1 lime
1 tbsp fresh oregano
1 tsp salt

1. Arrange all the vegetables on a baking sheet and drizzle with olive oil.
2. Roast vegetable in 400° oven until everything is nicely charred, about 10-15 min.
3. Remove seeds and stems from bell peppers and jalapenos, and peel as much skin as possible

off of peppers and tomatoes.
4. Add everything to a blender or food processor and blend until smooth.
5. Serve with almond flour chips or over braised meats!
Makes about 1 quart.

Salsa Verde

This sauce's name literally just means "green sauce", but the classic preparation relies on tart and juicy green tomatillos to give it it's unique flavor.

5-6 medium green tomatillos, husked and rinsed
1 jalapeno, sliced (leave ribs and seeds if you like it hot, if not remove them)
¼ cup fresh cilantro
¼ onion, diced
1 tbsp lime juice
salt, to taste

1. Add all ingredients to a blender or food processor and blend until smooth.
2. Swerve hot or cold on a variety of Latin dishes!
Makes about 1 cup.

Guacamole

Fresh guacamole is not only one of the tastiest thing you can possibly eat, it's also one of the healthiest. Avocados are loaded with good fats and a multitude of nutrients that Paleo people especially can appreciate!

2 ripe avocados
2 tbsp diced tomatoes
1 clove garlic, minced
¼ onion, minced
juice of ½ lime
1 tbsp fresh cilantro, chopped

1. Slice the avocados in half length-wise and twist to separate. Remove pit by striking with the sharp and of a knife and twisting.
2. Scoop meat from avocado into a medium mixing bowl.
3. Add remaining ingredients, making sure everything is finely chopped.
4. Stir with a fork, breaking up any chinks of avocado, until mixture is smooth.
5. Serve on chicken, beef, braised pork, with veggies or just eat it with a spoon!
Makes about 2 cups.

Chocolate Mole

Mole is one of the most complex and interesting sauces you will find south of the border. Most well known among this expansive family of sauces is chocolate mole, a sweet, bitter, and savory sauce that takes chicken and pork dishes to a whole new level.

Dark chocolate is another Paleo gray area, but cocoa powder is just a ground tree bean, and that simple substitution makes this classic recipe perfect.

5 dried ancho chiles
1 small onion, diced
1 clove garlic, minced
2 tbsp olive oil
¼ cup sliced almonds
2 large roma or plum tomatos, seeded and diced
¼ cup dark raisins
¾ tbsp salt
1 tsp black pepper
1 cup water (more as needed)
2 tbsp cocoa powder

¼ teaspoon each:
cinnamon
ground cloves
dried oregano
cumin
ground coriander
ground anise

1. Remove the seeds and stems from the chiles and rehydrate them in hot water for about 30 min.
2. Puree the softened chiles in a blender or food processor.
3. In a medium pan, sautee the garlic and onions until soft, about 3 min.
4. Add spices and herbs to the garlic and onions. Cook for 1 min, stirring constantly.
5. Add garlic/onion mixture to blender or food processor.
6. Add all remaining ingredients and blend until smooth.
7. Add more water if mixture is too thick.
8. Warm in a sauce pan before serving.
9. Serve over chicken or pork for a delicious gourmet Mexican meal!

Serves 2-4.

DRY RUBS AND SPICE MIXES

Sometimes all your eat needs is a little massage – with spices that is! Not only do dry rubs improve the flavor of your meat, but enough rubbing can actually improve the texture as well. Dry rubs can begin as simply as salt and pepper, and get as complex at the BBQ recipes we outlined a few chapters ago.

It should be noted that none of these recipes include instructions because all the instructions are the same: mix all ingredients together and rub vigorously onto your meat.

Cook your meat however you prefer and you've got dinner!

Basic BBQ Rub

This spicy rub is based on the original Kansas City style recipe, with a few tweaks.

2 tbsp salt
2 tbsp smoked paprika
2 tbsp roasted ground cumin
2 tbsp chipotle chili powder
1 tbsp garlic powder
1 tbsp onion powder
1 tbsp roasted ground coriander
1 tbsp ground mustard
1 tbsp red pepper flake
1 tbsp black pepper
2 tsp ground sage
2 tsp celery seed
1 tsp cayenne

Makes enough to cover a 2 lb roast or 1 whole chicken.

Tex-Mex Taco Seasoning

This taco spice mix turns any ground meat into Mexican food, and goes great on steaks and chicken too!

¼ cup roasted ground cumin
2 tbsp chipotle chili powder
2 tbsp salt
1 tbsp black pepper
1 tbsp onion powder
2 tsp paprika
1 tsp turmeric

Makes enough to generously season up to 2 lbs of ground meat or 1 whole chicken.

Mediterranean Herb Crust

This zesty herbaceous rub will add some zip to your favorite chicken, lamb or pork dishes.

1 tbsp salt
1 tbsp black pepper

2 tsp dried oregano
2 tsp dried thyme
2 tsp dried mint
1 tsp rubbed sage
1 tsp dried green onion (or finely minced fresh)
zest of 1 lemon

Makes enough to season a rack of lamb or 3-4 chicken breasts.

Asian Ginger Rub

This spicy mix of Asian inspired spices has a flavor all its own that goes perfect on chicken or beef.

2 tbsp dried ground ginger
2 tsp dried green onion (or finely chopped fresh)
2 tsp curry powder
1 tsp cinnamon
1 tsp ground anise
½ tsp ground clove
½ tsp ground allspice
zest of 1 lime

Makes enough to season 2-3 steaks or chicken breasts.

Spicy Chili Rub

This fiery rub is all about bringing the heat! A great base for chili too with the addition of ground beef.

¼ cup chipotle chili powder
2 tbsp salt
1 tbsp black pepper
1 tbsp cumin
1 tbsp paprika
2 tsp cayenne
2 tsp red pepper flake

Makes enough to season a 2 lb roast that will make you stand up and shout!

PARTY DIPS

Wherever there's a party, there's bound to be dip or two, and that's true even in the Paleo world! With a little creativity, it's not that hard to replicate some party classics, or even to make up some new creations of your own.

The dips featured in this chapter are primal spins on classic party dips that will keep even your non-Paleo guests happy.

Sour Cream and Onion Dip

For those who tolerate dairy, sour cream may be on the menu occasionally. But for those who don't, this little trick is here to save the day!

- 1 14 oz. can full-fat coconut milk
- 1-2 tbsp lemon juice or apple cider vinegar
- ¼ tsp salt
- 2-3 green onions, sliced thin
- 1 tsp black pepper
- 1 tsp dill weed

1. Leave the can of coconut milk in the refrigerator overnight. The cream will separate from the milk and harden.
2. Open the can from the BOTTOM. This allows you to pour out the milk and leaves you with only the fat.
3. Scoop the fat into a small mixing bowl.
4. Stir in lemon juice or vinegar and salt. Taste, add more if desired. You now have Paleo sour cream!
5. Stir in remaining ingredients.
6. Serve with celery or almond flour chips.

Makes about 1 cup.

Multi-Nut Butter

Nut butters are a great, mildly sweet appetizer to set out at parties. Everyone is sure to love this recipe, whether it's on vegetables or homemade crackers!

- 1 cup roasted cashews
- 1 cup roasted almonds
- ½ cup roasted pecans
- ½ cup roasted walnuts
- ¼ cup sunflower seeds
- ¼ cup pumpkin seeds
- 1 tbsp grapeseed oil
- 2 tsp salt
- ½ tsp cinnamon
- ¼ tsp ground allspice
- ¼ tsp ground nutmeg

1. Place all ingredients in a food processor and blend until smooth. This will take some time, so be patient.
2. Serve alongside celery, carrots and jicama.

Makes about 3 cups.

Paleo Ranch Dip

Here's where some of those foundational recipes way back in the first chapter are going to start paying off. Who throws a party without ranch dip? No one, that's who!

½ cup Paleo Mayo
½ cup Paleo Sour Cream (consult the Sour Cream recipe in chapter 1 for how to make this)
1 clove garlic, finely minced
¼ cup fresh parsley, chopped
1 tbsp clarified butter
2 tsp black pepper
1 tsp dill weed
1 tsp onion powder

1. Stir all ingredients together in a mixing bowl.
2. Serve with raw celery, carrots, broccoli, cauliflower and cherry tomatoes.

Makes about 1 cup.

Paleo Hummus

Oh yes, it's real! Thanks to a clever substitution, hummus is back on the menu, even though beans and legumes are off!

1 cup raw cashews
¼ cup tahini
2 cloves garlic
juice of two lemons
1 tbsp olive oil
½ tsp salt
¾ tsp cumin
¼ cup coconut milk

1. Submerge the cashews in water and soak in the refrigerator overnight.
2. Remove cashews from refrigerator, rinse thoroughly and drain.
3. Add cashews, tahini and garlic cloves to a food processor and blend until a thick paste forms.
4. Ass lemon juice, olive oil, salt and cumin. Blend until well incorporated.
5. Add coconut milk 1 tbsp at a time until desired texture is reached.
6. Serve with raw zucchini for dipping. Top with a drizzle of olive oil and a sprinkle of paprika if desired.

Makes about 1½ cups.

Pimento Cheese

If you're from the south, you know pimento cheese! It's a distinctly southern dip/condiment that goes great with cured meats like ham, in eggs or on crackers.

2 cups shredded sharp cheddar
8 oz. cream cheese, room temperature OR ½ Paleo mayo
½ cup Paleo mayo
¼ tsp garlic powder
¼ tsp cayenne (optional)
¼ tsp onion powder
1 4 oz. jar diced pimento, drained
salt and pepper to taste

1. Mix all ingredients in a mixing bowl.
2. Serve with homemade almond crackers, or on nut-crusted fried green tomatoes!

Makes about 3 cups

SALAD DRESSINGS

We've finally come to it – the multifaceted world of salad dressing.

We paleo people make a lot of things from scratch – it comes with the territory. But salad dressing is one of those things that, though it seems daunting at first, you will want to make yourself from now on. whether you stay Paleo or not. Once you've made fresh, homemade salad dressing from quality ingredients, the processed store bought stuff starts tasting like garbage.

There are so many salad dressings out there that to try to include a Paleo version of all of them – or even just the classic ones – would take a book of its own. Here, we've presented a healthy roundup of the classics, as well as an assortment of creative vinaigrettes and new creations. Whatever you put in your salad, there's bound to be something in here you like.

Ranch

It's everyone's favorite dressing, and it's no wonder why! This rich and creamy dressing goes great on everything from lettuce to pizza, and we're remaking it Paleo-style!

½ cup Paleo mayo
¼ cup coconut milk
¼ cup water
1 tbsp clarified butter, melted
1 clove garlic, finely minced
¼ cup fresh parsley, chopped
2 tsp black pepper
1 tsp dill weed
1 tsp onion powder

1. Add all ingredients to a food processor and blend until smooth.
2. Serve on salads or drizzled on roasted veggies.

Makes about 1 cup.

Balsamic Vinaigrette

This is probably everyone's *second* favorite dressing. The slight sweetness and tanginess of balsamic vinegar makes a great addition to any salad.

½ cup balsamic vinegar
½ cup olive oil
2 tsp dried basil
2 tsp dried oregano
2 tsp dried thyme
2 clove garlic, minced
2 tsp black pepper
1 pinch salt

1. Add all ingredients to a food processor and blend until smooth.
2. Serve over spring mix or drizzled over fresh strawberries.

Makes about 1 cup.

Greek Dressing

We enter the gray zone again here with the addition of feta cheese, but this dressing is worth a try even if you don't usually eat cheese!

½ cup olive oil
¼ cup white wine vinegar
2 cloves garlic, minced
1 tbsp fresh basil, chopped
1 tbsp fresh oregano, chopped
1 tbsp fresh mint, chopped
2 tbsp feta cheese
¼ cup Kalamata olives, pitted

1. Add all ingredients to a food processor and blend until smooth.
2. Serve over a lettuce salad with cucumbers, tomatoes and sliced red onion.

Makes about 1 cup.

Zesty Italian

This classic can be seen everywhere from pizza parlors to upscale restaurants, and it's no wonder why. It makes great salad!

This recipe uses raw honey – another Paleo gray area. Our conclusion is that the occasional drift into a gray area won't hurt, as long as it's small – and worth it.

½ cup olive oil
½ cup red wine vinegar
2 tbsp water
1 tsp garlic powder
1 tsp onion powder
1 tsp fresh oregano, chopped
1 tsp fresh thyme, chopped
1 tsp fresh basil, chopped
1 tsp fresh parsley, chopped
1 tbsp raw honey (optional, but recommended)

1. Add all ingredients to a food processor and blend until smooth.
2. Serve over an iceberg wedge or in a cucumber and tomato salad with black olives.

Makes about 1 cup.

Caesar

Did we say balsamic was the second favorite? Well this one has got to be tied for second place. The creamy, cheesy tang of a classic Caesar salad is not something anyone – even a Paleo dieter – should go without.

6 anchovy filets (packed in oil)
1 clove garlic
1 pinch salt
2 egg yolks
2 tbsp lemon juice

½ tsp Dijon mustard
2 tbsp olive oil
½ cup grapeseed oil
3 tbsp finely grated Parmesan
½ tsp black pepper

1. Chop anchovies, garlic and salt and mash into a paste using the side of a knife. Transfer to a mixing bowl.
2. Add egg yolks, lemon juice and Dijon.
3. Whisk until smooth.
4. Mix both oils together in a measuring cup for easy pouring.
5. Slowly, drop by drop, add oil to egg mixture, whisking constantly.
6. When all oil is added, whisk in Parmesan and black pepper. Add more salt or lemon juice if desired.
7. Serve over hearts of romaine with baked Parmesan crisps for that classic flavor and texture!

Makes about 1 cup.

Raspberry Vinaigrette

If you're looking for a sweet and tangy option to top a salad full of savory veggies, raspberry vinaigrette is probably your first thought. This recipe is super-easy and everyone is sure to love it.

½ cup grapeseed oil
¼ cup red wine vinegar
½ cup fresh raspberries
1 tsp black pepper
1 pinch salt

1. Add all ingredients to a food processor and blend until smooth.
2. Run mixture through a mesh strainer to remove seeds and solids. Press with a rubber spatula for faster results.
3. Serve over a spring green salad with dried strawberries and red onion.

Makes about 1 cup.

Strawberry Basil Balsamic Vinaigrette

Strawberries, fresh basil and balsamic vinegar are so good together you could just eat them plain. In a dressing, over some butter lettuce? Heaven.

1 cup fresh strawberries, tops removed and thoroughly rinsed
½ cup grapeseed oil
¼ cup balsamic vinegar
¼ cup fresh basil, packed
1 tsp black pepper
1 pinch salt

1. Add all ingredients to a food processor and blend until smooth.
2. Run mixture through a mesh strainer to remove seeds and solids. Press with a rubber spatula for faster results.

3. Serve over soft butter or Boston lettuce with cucumbers and shaved onion.
Makes about 1 cup.

Blueberry Thyme Vinaigrette

This little number is a riff on the last recipe, with a few interesting switches.

1 cup fresh blueberries, thoroughly rinsed
½ cup olive oil
¼ cup red wine vinegar
¼ cup fresh thyme
1 tsp black pepper
1 pinch salt

1. Add all ingredients to a food processor and blend until smooth.
2. Run mixture through a mesh strainer to remove seeds and skins. Press with a rubber spatula for faster results.
3. Serve over bitter greens with cantaloupe chunks and pumpkin seeds.
Makes about 1 cup.

Primal Green Goddess Dressing

This spin on the salad bar classic uses creamy avocado and a blast of fresh herbs to create a wonderful, hearty addition to any salad.

½ ripe avocado
¼ cup grapeseed oil
½ cup coconut milk
½ cup fresh basil
¼ cup fresh oregano
¼ cup fresh sage
¼ cup fresh mint
¼ cup fresh tarragon
2 green onions, chopped
1 tsp salt
1 tsp black pepper.

1. Add all ingredients to a food processor and blend until herbs are chopped and consistency is smooth.
2. Serve over a hearty salad of mixed vegetables and seeds. It even goes great on beef!
Makes about 1½ cups.

Thai Coleslaw Dressing

This creamy and spicy mixture turns shredded cabbage into an exotic southeast Asian slaw.

½ cup coconut milk
½ cup Paleo mayo
1 jalapeno, ribs and seeds removed

¼ cup fresh basil (Thai basil, if you can get it)
¼ cup fresh cilantro
Juice and zest of one lemon
Juice and zest of one lime
1 tsp ground coriander
1 tsp black pepper
1 tsp salt

1. Add all ingredients to a food processor and blend until smooth.
2. Pour over shredded cabbage and carrots for a spicy, exotic slaw!

Juicy Citrus Dressing

This fruity concoction is a friend to all salads, both fruit and vegetable. The sweetness from the orange and the tanginess form the lemon and lime are a perfect combination.

Juice of 2 oranges
Zest of 1 orange
Juice and zest of 1 lemon
Juice and zest of 1 lime
½ cup grapeseed oil
1 tbsp apple cider vinegar
1 tbsp fresh parsley, chopped
Salt and pepper to taste

1. Add all ingredients to a food processor and blend until smooth.
2. Serve drizzled over mangoes and strawberries for a gourmet treat.

Makes about 1 cup.

Thousand Island

Thousand Island might not be for everybody, but there are those who are addicted to it! Goes great anywhere ranch is welcome – even pizza!

½ cup Paleo mayo
½ cup Paleo ketchup (didn't we say the basics would come in handy?)
2 tbsp finely chopped, all-natural dill pickles
2 tsp finely chopped onion
1 tsp black pepper

1. Mix all ingredients in a mixing bowl until smooth.
2. Serve on salad or spread over roast beef with sauerkraut for a Paleo Reuben!

Makes about 1 cup.

Roasted Red Pepper Dressing

This smoky delicious dressing is a little different than what you may be used to, but served over shredded romaine with diced chicken, it's a dish unto itself.

1 red bell pepper
1 shallot
1 clove garlic
½ cup plus 2 tbsp olive oil
2 tbsp red wine vinegar
1 tsp black pepper
1 tsp salt

1. Arrange the pepper, shallot and garlic on a baking sheet and drizzle with olive oil.
2. Roast in a 400° oven until everything is nicely charred, about 10 min.
3. Remove stem and seeds from pepper and cut any roots off the onion.
4. Under cold running water, peel all skin off of pepper.
5. Add all ingredients to a food processor and blend until smooth.
6. Serve over a bitter green salad with grilled mahi mahi.

Makes about 1 cup.

Ginger Almond Dressing

This Asian-inspired dressing is sure to satisfy those cravings for nutty dressings!

¼ cup almond butter
½ cup grapeseed oil
1/8 tsp sesame oil (optional)
¼ cup coconut aminos
2 tsp grated fresh ginger
1 pinch cinnamon
salt and pepper to taste

1. Add all ingredients to a food processor and blend until smooth.
2. Serve over a lettuce salad with shaved carrot and daikon radish.

Makes about 1 cup.

Honey Pecan Dressing

This decadent dressing dabbles in the gray areas again, but when you're craving some seriously sweet dressing over a salad with lots of fruits and nuts, this is your new go-to!

¼ cup roasted pecans
¼ cup plus 2 tbsp raw honey
½ cup grapeseed oil
1 tbsp apple cider vinegar
1 pinch salt

1. Add all ingredients to a food processor and blend until rich and creamy.
2. Serve over a lettuce salad with toasted walnuts and fresh strawberries.

Makes about 1 cup.

Made in the USA
San Bernardino, CA
02 September 2014